KING CAMP GILLETTE

1855-1932

First published in 2001 by
Short Books
15 Highbury Terrace
London N5 1UP

A CIP catalogue record for this book
is available from the British Library.

ISBN 0 571 20810 X

Printed in Great Britain by
Bookmarque Ltd, Croydon, Surrey

INVENTOR OF THE DISPOSABLE CULTURE

KING CAMP GILLETTE
1855-1932

TIM DOWLING

SHORT BOOKS

For my father

King C Gillette

IN A NOTE DATED 26 DECEMBER 2000, the author Edward Bellamy reminds his readers that modern American society, a system 'at once so simple and so logical that it seems but the triumph of common sense', is, remarkably, less than 100 years old.

This Boxing Day tribute to the status quo is not all it seems. Bellamy actually wrote these words in 1887, in the preface to his utopian novel *Looking Backward*, the story of a young Bostonian, Julian West, who falls into a trance and wakes in the year 2000, where he is able to see first-hand how the problems which plagued late 19th-century America have been overcome. Technology has rescued mankind from drudgery. There are no prisons or labour strikes, and everyone is treated equally, regardless of status or contribution. As West's guide to the future, the kindly Dr Leete explains, 'The title of every man, woman, and child to the means of existence rests on no basis less plain, broad, and simple than the fact that they are fellows of one race – members of one human family.'

First published in 1888, *Looking Backward* became one of the biggest-selling books of the 19th century. Its success

spawned Nationalist clubs dedicated to the implemen-
tation of Bellamy's vision, Nationalist magazines (one,
the *New Nation*, edited by Bellamy himself) and a
political party, as well as a small industry in utopian and
anti-utopian literature. Dozens of imitations, responses,
improvements and sequels were published, with titles like
Looking Forward, *Looking Further Backward*, *Looking
Further Forward*, *Looking Ahead*, *Looking Beyond* and,
inevitably, *Looking Within*.

At the end of the last century America perceived itself
as being at a crossroads. The country was expanding
rapidly, even as the frontiers were closing. Widespread
strikes, massive industrial growth and a wholly unreg-
ulated stock market meant that economic instability was
the norm. As an uncertain future beckoned, many more
utopias were committed to print. Some, like *Looking
Backward*, were fictional; others were serious proposals
for new forms of society, practical schemes to erect an
egalitarian paradise out of the chaos of the present. One
such blueprint, a slim paperback volume entitled *The
Human Drift*, appeared in late 1894. Its author was a
travelling salesman from Boston with the unlikely name of
King Camp Gillette.

The Human Drift proposed a collective, co-operative
society similar to the one in *Looking Backward*, where
increased efficiency would ensure that people would be

required to work for only five years of their lives, from the ages of 25 to 30. The author also envisaged the entire population living in a single, purpose-built city powered by the Niagara Falls: 60 million people housed in 40,000 towering skyscrapers, and eating together in massive central dining halls serving 1,500 at a time. Explanatory plates and detailed illustrations of this 'Metropolis' accompanied the text. The world of utopian literature was full of outlandish schemes and predictions which approached the level of parody, but no reader of *The Human Drift* could doubt that King Gillette was utterly in earnest.

A portrait of the author on the book's title-page shows a youngish man wearing a white tie and wing collar, with black curly hair and a neat moustache. His cheeks are smooth and ample, although the pale eyes are prematurely bagged, perhaps a consequence of too many late nights spent tinkering, for the man had for many years been an obsessive inventor – he already had several patents to his name. The photograph does not show that he was a large, imposing figure; nor can it convey that he was loquacious, even garrulous, with a beguiling manner that few who met him failed to remark upon. He was also not quite as young as the picture might lead his readers to believe. At the time of the book's publication he was just weeks away from his 40th birthday.

The book represented something of a mid-life *cri de coeur* for King Gillette: as an inventor he had never enjoyed much success, and he was aware that the new technologies of the coming century were beyond his limited understanding of mechanics and basic engineering. At the time the country was in the grip of the worst depression in its history, brought on by unchecked speculation and a currency panic; Gillette's faith in America as a land of boundless opportunity had been badly undermined. And yet it was also a time of great hope, perhaps best evinced by the tremendous enthusiasm surrounding the 1893 Chicago World's Fair, with its electric kitchen, its moving sidewalks and its dazzling, neo-classical 'White City'. While the new century held considerable promise, it was clear to Gillette that the old order – the wasteful, cut-throat lottery of the capital-driven economy – was no longer supportable. Along with many other men and women of his generation, King Gillette had dared to imagine a radically different future, and he believed he had discovered a path to it.

With the publication of *The Human Drift*, Gillette embarked on what he thought would be his life's work, as nothing less than the saviour of mankind. His scheme, if acted upon, would usher in a new era of unparalleled human achievement. In fact, within a decade, the name King Gillette would come to encapsulate a rather more traditional American Dream, one of Yankee ingenuity, entrepreneurial daring and material reward. Gillette would be remembered not as the founder of a brave new world, but as a standard-bearer of mass-market capitalism and the progenitor of the notion of disposability.

The man who wanted to change the world would have to be content to be known as the man who changed the way the world shaved.

**

King Camp Gillette was born in Wisconsin on 5 January 1855. There is a rather mundane explanation for his singular name. 'King' was the surname of a family friend, and Camp was Gillette's mother's maiden name. Gillette's parents both came from old New England families whose pioneering spirit had carried their ancestors westward. Gillette's mother, Fannie Lemira Camp, was said to be the first child born in Ann Arbor, Michigan, by which it was meant she was the first white child born there – the area was already well-populated with Indians. After graduating from the Albion Seminary at the age of 19, she moved with her family to the even more remote outpost of Sheboygan, Wisconsin, where she met George Wolcott Gillette, the young owner-editor of the weekly *Sheboygan Mercury* and a sometime correspondent for the New York *Tribune*. They married in 1848, and had five children:

Lina, Mott, George, King and Fanny. By the time of King Gillette's birth the family had moved still further west, to Fond du Lac, a settlement on the shores of Lake Winnebago. However, Fond du Lac soon proved too small for the industrious George Gillette, and a few years after the railroad first came north he took his family south to Chicago.

The Gillette children were educated in the Chicago public schools during and just after the Civil War, which ended when King was ten. Of his schooldays Gillette would later write, 'My father's business at that time was the manufacturing and selling of a patented invention of his own. My two older brothers were in business with him.' In fact, Gillette's father went into business as a manufacturer of 'japanned tinware'; he also held the rights to a 'machine for making screws' invented by a local machinist named Treat T Prosser. It was not until 1873 that George Gillette received his first patent, as co-inventor (with Prosser) of a 'tool for facing bungholes'. But by the time this patent was granted, he was already ruined.

At nine o'clock on the evening of Sunday 8 October 1871, the Gillette family were comfortably settled in their home on West Randolph Street, in Chicago's West Division. The evening's conversation would have been dominated by the previous night's big fire, which destroyed four square blocks of an adjacent neighborhood, and had only been put out that afternoon. The younger children, King and Fanny, had school the next day and went to bed unaware that another fire was already burning 15 blocks south, ignited, so the legend goes, when Mrs O'Leary's cow kicked over a lantern. Fanned by a stiff southwesterly wind, the flames quickly spread towards the centre of Chicago, a city built largely of timber (even the streets were paved with wood). By midnight the conflagration had crossed the greasy river into the main business district. From there it surged towards the North Side, burning all Monday and throughout the night, finally dying out as rain began to fall early on Tuesday morning. The Great Chicago Fire killed at least 300 people and left 100,000 homeless. The Gillette family home was safely west of the devastation, but George Gillette's business lay directly in the path of the fire. Like so many others, he lost everything.

Chicago would go on to make a quick and remarkable recovery, but it would do so without George Gillette, who relocated his family to New York's Upper West Side and set up a hardware business with his older sons. Only King, now 17, stayed behind. He took a job as a clerk with the Chicago hardware wholesalers Seeberger & Breakey, becoming, as he put it, 'the pilot of my own destiny'. He worked hard, and was soon offered a new job with a New

York hardware firm. By the age of 21 he had been promoted to what was then called a 'commercial traveler', selling hardware across the country and spending most of his time in hotels and railway carriages, in the days when the trip from New York to Chicago took 26 hours.

His schooling cut short by circumstance, King Gillette now received his real education, on the road, as one of the younger 'drummers' criss-crossing the United States by train. It was regarded as a rather romantic life, providing an opportunity to make a good living, which appealed to many a young man stuck behind a desk or a shop counter. An 1889 pamphlet, plainly titled *How To Be Successful on the Road as a Commercial Traveler, by an Old Drummer*, cautioned those who might be 'carried away with the imaginary charms and attractions of "going on the road", being perhaps under the illusion that they have the necessary requirements for a successful traveler'.

Undoubtedly, the young King Gillette had all the necessary requirements, and he took care to look the part: fastidious but not foppish; businesslike, but not too austere. He oiled his curly hair and parted it neatly in the centre. He also wore a moustache, which made him look older. His biggest asset, though, was his magnetism; an almost hypnotic cloak of easy-going, clubbable charm. He possessed what the Old Drummer called 'a certain pleasing and winning expression of countenance, which some persons who otherwise can make no pretensions to personal beauty, possess to such an extent that it is almost impossible to resist their fascinations'. This was young King Gillette to a tee – more handsome in person than photographs could capture, and preternaturally persuasive. Though he spoke softly, it was in a manner that commanded attention: he looked his customers in the eye, used their names, touched their sleeves, adapted himself to their opinions and prejudices. Above all, he sold himself. The formality of taking an order could wait.

Not that selling consumed him entirely. Even as a young man, Gillette had other ambitions. Invention was a family tradition, and in his spare moments he constantly tinkered with the bits of hardware in his sample box, his mind bent on improving their design. 'My impulse to think and invent was a natural one,' he said later, 'as it was with my father and brothers – as will be found in looking over the records of the patent office where there are a great many inventions to our credit.'

The records show that King Gillette's first patent was granted on 2 December 1879, a month before his 25th birthday, for an improved wooden bushing for beer barrels. An ordinary bushing – the collar lining the bunghole of a barrel – tended to become misshapen and enlarged in the course of a barrel's life, as one faucet after another was driven into it with a mallet, 'oftentimes with much unnecessary violence' according to Gillette's patent. His sturdy, cross-grained bushing was just one of a number of innovations which amounted to a collective inventive assault by the Gillette brothers on the beer barrel, an object they clearly felt was in want of considerable refinement. That same year King's brother, George, patented a 'bung bush expander' and his brother, Mott, invented a new tap valve. In October King himself filed a patent for a 'tap and bushing valve combined', a system in which the valve opened only when the faucet was fully engaged, 'thus obviating all waste of liquid on tapping'. In 1883 George designed a metal-skinned barrel; the next year George Sr patented a tap vent, and in 1886 Mott developed a method for constructing barrels. Despite this concentration of effort – and the brief formation of a family concern, the Gillette Tap Valve and Faucet Company – none of these inventions was destined to set the world alight; most of the patents ended up in the hands of various assignees. According to King Gillette his barrel improvements 'made money for others, but seldom for myself'.

The American passion for inventing, which began with Eli Whitney's cotton gin in 1794, had for Gillette's generation become something of a national craze. During the Civil War between 3,000 and 4,000 patents were granted annually, but in the decade after General Lee's surrender in

1865 the rate was more than 12,000 per year, almost three times the UK average for the same period. By 1885 the total number of patents granted had topped 300,000 – 34,697 US patent applications were filed that year alone. At different stages in their lives both Abraham Lincoln and Mark Twain were granted patents (Lincoln's, issued ten years before he became President, was for a system for 'buoying boats over shoals'; Twain received three – for a type of suspenders, a game and a 'self-pasting scrapbook'). The Gillette brothers were among the many who, wisely or foolishly, sought to make their fortunes through inventing, trusting in Ralph Waldo Emerson's dictum that, if a man can only make a better mousetrap than his neighbour, 'the world will make a beaten path to his door'. The reality was more uncertain. Many of the inventions patented were impractical or useless. Frivolous devices like the 'combined finger ring and tooth pick' (1883) or the 1879 'fire escape' (an outsize parachute hat, used with rubber shoes) competed for space in the *Patent Gazette* with the Gillette brothers' sober little improvements. Many worthy inventions failed because of a lack of investment, or drove their originators into bankruptcy. Inventing required, as it still does, heroic measures of perseverance and self-belief, and a tremendous capacity for disappointment. 'There is no hope,' Gillette said, 'like that which springs eternal in the mind of the inventor.'

At this stage the only real success of the family was Gillette's mother, Fannie, who in 1887 published a best-selling cookbook. During the early days of her marriage in rough and ready Wisconsin, Fannie Gillette had been embarrassed by her ignorance of cooking and house-keeping, and had set about correcting this fault with a thoroughness she would pass on to her sons, collecting, compiling and testing recipes over three decades. The result was called *The White House Cookbook*. A strange mixture of the homespun and the highfalutin – the book includes a menu for a 'buffet for 1,000 people', as well as the advice that 'sufferers from asthma should get a muskrat skin and wear it over their lungs' – it sold millions and was reprinted many times. And so it was that, of all the enterprising and ambitious Gillettes, Fannie became the first to be listed in *Who's Who*.

Her son King, meanwhile, had switched jobs again, becoming a salesman for Enoch Morgan's Sons Co of New York, the manufacturers of Sapolio, a popular abra-sive scouring soap made from tallow and finely ground quartz. The Morgans' pioneering advertising manager Artemas Ward had already turned Sapolio into one of the first nationally known trademarks, and now it was to become an international brand. King Gillette was dispatched to London to sell soap.

In his absence Gillette's brothers continued to file

patents as assiduously as ever, but their search for a lucrative invention became rather unfocused. Mott worked on another improved tap valve with a new partner. George designed a paper fruit basket, assigning the patent rights to the Newark Paper Basket Company. Mott then patented a drawer-pull, and yet another barrel improvement. King must have returned from London sometime in late 1888, for, in January 1889, he and his brother George patented a type of electrical insulation made of interlocking glass segments. But he was soon forced to put inventing aside by the more pressing need to earn a living.

On 2 July 1890, the 35-year-old King Gillette married 21-year-old Alanta Ella Gaines, the daughter of an Ohio oilman. She was five months pregnant and later that year, in Ohio, Mrs Gillette gave birth to a son, who was christened King Gaines Gillette. King Sr settled his new family in New York City, but soon returned to the roads and rails in order to provide for them.

Over the years Gillette had developed a reputation as a good salesman, and in 1891 he was invited to join the ranks of a new enterprise, the Baltimore Bottle Seal Company. In its small factory on Monument Street in Baltimore, the company manufactured a little rubber disk with a canvas facing on one side and a ring-pull on the other: an economical – and disposable – bottle stopper which was already revolutionising the bottling industry.

Previously, drinks manufacturers and brewers had bottled their own product using a variety of stoppers, corks and seals, sometimes under questionable sanitary conditions. The bottle seal was the brainchild of William Painter, a co-founder of the company and a prodigious inventor who had some 85 patents to his name, ranging from pumps for emptying cesspools to counterfeit-coin detectors. He and Gillette quickly became friends. Whenever business brought Gillette to Baltimore, he would stay with Painter at his home in the city; and during these visits the pair would spend hours discussing the nature of innovation, with the boss naturally doing most of the talking, and his employee most of the listening.

A year after Gillette joined the Bottle Seal Company, Painter patented a new sealing device: the 'Crown Cork' – a cork-lined, crimped metal stopper virtually identical to the modern bottle cap. The crown cork quickly became popular with bottlers as an economical and reliably airtight seal. It was also gratifyingly disposable: once removed it could not be used to reseal the bottle, encouraging immediate consumption of the contents.

'King,' Painter exclaimed to his friend one day, 'you are always thinking and inventing something. Why don't you try to think of something like the crown cork, which, once used, is thrown away, and the customer keeps coming back for more – and with every additional customer you get, you are building a foundation for profit?'

The terrible ear for dialogue is characteristic of most of Gillette's reminiscences, but he never forgot Painter's advice. Gillette's previous inventions, practical though they were, had generally been sturdier versions of existing devices, built to last or to minimise waste. The success of Painter's throwaway bottle cap fundamentally changed his thinking.

***

It was on a business trip to Scranton, Pennsylvania, in 1889 that King Gillette first hit upon his most revolutionary idea – the one which would change his life, or so he thought – while staring out of a hotel window. The name of the hotel is lost to history, although *How To Be Successful on the Road as a Commercial Traveler* recommends the Wyoming as the best in Scranton. On that fateful day the sky was black with cloud, and a stiff wind drove sheets of rain along the muddy, rutted street outside. Unable to make his appointed sales calls in town, Gillette was glowering at the weather and fidgeting in unaccustomed idleness when he was suddenly struck by enlightenment.

Recalling the moment 17 years later, he wrote, 'As I sat at the hotel window, watching the passing of man and beast as they waded through wet and mud, there came a sudden halt in the procession of street cars generally. Men and women with umbrellas congregated at the curb to note the breakdown of a truck loaded with groceries. I watched the excitement and confusion incident to this stopping of traffic, and began to turn over in my mind the thought of improvement.'

As an aspiring inventor, Gillette was in the regular habit of examining everything with an eye towards making refinements which might, in turn, make his fortune. This time, however, he conceived a scheme not to improve the way trucks were designed, or roads surfaced, or goods delivered. He had something far more radical in mind. Looking at the truck, he followed it in his mind back to the warehouse, 'then taking up the burden of products followed them to the mills, factories and other places where raw materials had been converted into finished products. I traced the flour from the mills to the farmer, the salt to the earth, the sugar to the plantations, the spices across the seas to China and Japan, the coffee to Brazil and in all my reasoning, in all my mental travels, *I found one vast connected mechanism...*'

The more Gillette thought, the more he began to see all the industrial, economic, political and social systems of the world to be parts of a single machine. And that machine, to his mind, was broken. For a man who spent much of his time absorbed in the intricacies of small fragments of hardware, this cloudless vista of inter-connectedness was a revelation. His solution, though revolutionary, was straightforward: 'The task I set myself was this: first, to discover a practical, businesslike method, whereby people might gradually absorb and eventually come into complete possession of the world and its wealth. Second, to organise society under the new system, that equity, justice and freedom would be guarantied to each and every individual.'

King Gillette's political influences, if indeed he had any, are unknown. Certainly, growing up in Chicago, with its tradition of innovation and labour radicalism, must have been an education. Gillette's personal philosophy, however, was forged not on the picket line but in the Pullman car, where the complex problems of capital and labour were daily solved by men without a significant stake in either, the 'nomadic fraternity' of commercial travellers.

'It is to this class that I am largely indebted,' said Gillette, 'in their endorsement of my view that the drift of commercial affairs is moving with constantly accelerating force toward a common focus.' Rolling towards their next destination, Gillette and his fellow drummers would speak their minds to each other in a way they never dared to do with customers, dissecting the latest railroad strike, the recent currency crisis, each new merger and bankruptcy.

They extolled the marvels of the Chicago World's Fair, which an awe-struck Gillette visited, along with 22 million others, in the summer of 1893. They debated the merits of the gold standard versus 'bimetallism'. They weighed up the influence of the various political factions – Greenbackers, Socialists, Stalwarts, Prohibitionists, Populists, Half-Breeds, Mugwumps – at work within and without the two main parties. They discussed *Looking Backward*, the biggest-selling book since *Uncle Tom's Cabin*. Most of all they expounded on the wide-open subject of what might happen *next*. And, after several years of high-level dining-car consultation, Gillette was moved to set out his own conclusions in print.

***

On a chilly New York afternoon a few days before Christmas 1894, the editor of the radical weekly journal *Twentieth Century* walked into his offices on Astor Place to find another heap of mail spilling across his desk. Wearily he sorted the envelopes into piles without opening them; he could distinguish easily enough between articles commissioned and unsolicited, between letters angry and supportive, between subscription renewals (with cheques) and pledges to the magazine's erstwhile co-operative movement (without). Only one parcel, postmarked in Boston, remained a mystery. Inside was a paperback, inscrutably titled *The Human Drift*. The book proved impossible to judge by its cover, an illustration of a globe swathed in a banner reading 'United Intelligence and Material Equality': was this socialism, or science fiction? He had never heard of its author, or the publishers, but this little volume was better got up than many he received. A predictably turgid tone of *fin-de-siècle* foreboding was evident even on the title page – '*There are clouds upon the horizon of thought, and the very air we breathe is pregnant with life that foretells the birth of a wonderful change*' – but as the editor read further he found himself becoming improbably engrossed, until finally the hairs on the back of his neck stood up. A complete stranger from Boston had somehow read his mind.

Twentieth Century was associated with the Bellamy Nationalist cause (it had subsumed Bellamy's the *New Nation* the previous year), and the editor had recently formed a movement to secure a future like the one described in *Looking Backward*. Until now he had modelled it on the socialist Laurence Gronlund's book, *The Cooperative Commonwealth*. Now, however, he had more than a model. He had a blueprint, a pragmatic business plan to rescue a cause which had been too long mired in apocalyptic generalities and wishful thinking: *The Human Drift* by King C Gillette.

The 'drift' of human history, as Mr Gillette saw it, was

moving inexorably towards the consolidation of industry into a single all-powerful entity. This was a rather commonplace theory at the end of the 19th century, no more original than Gillette's assessment of the competitive system as the root cause of 'murder, robbery, lying, prostitution, forgery, divorce, deception, brutality, ignorance, injustice, drunkenness, insanity, suicide, and every other crime'.

The inflammatory language was understandable. Gillette had penned his manuscript in the full force of the Panic of 1893, a currency crisis which had plunged the nation into the worst depression it had ever known: two and a half million people were unemployed, one in six railroads was operating in receivership, and hundreds of banks had shut their doors. President Cleveland's response was particularly heavy-handed – one railroad strike was crushed with federal troops – but few expected charity from politicians. 'Neither the Republican nor Democratic Party will ever aid the working men,' wrote Gillette, echoing a common sentiment. 'These parties are wedded to boodle, and managed and controlled in the interests of capital.'

If Gillette believed the rule of big capital was a foregone conclusion, he nevertheless admired the huge monopolies, or 'trusts', which controlled America's steel, coal, sugar, tobacco and barbed-wire industries. Despite their well-known crimes (slashing wages, fixing prices and engineering shortages to name a few), Gillette regarded the trusts as perfect economic machines, beyond the reach of government or legislation, and he took them as models for his new civilisation.

Under the banner 'United Intelligence and Material Equality', he proposed a gigantic trust owned by the people. He believed that lasting reform could only succeed if deployed under the auspices of accepted business methods – his 'United Company' was to be a sheep in wolf's clothing, first entering the grocery trade, then absorbing or destroying every other business in existence until it took control of the production and distribution of everything, by the people and for the people.

The ultimate 'centralisation' of industry would also have profound geographical consequences: 'Under a perfect economic system of production and distribution', wrote Gillette, 'there can only be one city on a continent, and possibly only one in the world.' This giant city, called 'Metropolis', would be situated along the shores of Lake Ontario, close to Niagara Falls, in order to take advantage of this natural wonder's potential as a source of hydroelectric power. The 60 million residents of Metropolis (90 per cent of the US population in 1894) would live in 40,000 circular, 25-storey apartment buildings of Gillette's own design. Beneath the buildings, the city would operate on three tiers, with the lowest devoted to electrical, water and sewage systems, the next to transportation, and the topmost reserved for a honeycomb of boulevards and manicured lawns. At common distribution centres would be displayed all manner of consumer goods. There would be no money. People could come and take what they wanted.

'I believe, as much as I believe that I live', wrote Gillette, 'that if the plan outlined could be understood by the masses, enthusiasm would amount to such a pitch in the excitement and desire to see Metropolis completed

Plan of building shown by the author in *The Human Drift*, published in 1894

that millions would enlist their services for an indefinite time to forward its building, and all they would ask would be soldier's fare and clothing. What would be money to them, when the near future would see it pass into the oblivion of an ignorant age?'

By the time he had completed his book, Gillette had moved his family from New York to Boston, the hub of his new sales territory. There, he financed its publication with the help of a friend, Ward Holloway, and sent a copy to *Twentieth Century*. Within days he was corresponding with the editor about putting the plan into action. Throughout the winter ecstatic reviews of *The Human Drift* appeared in the magazine. 'Hail to thy birth, *United People's Company*!' read one. 'Hail to the mind who conceived thee!'

Not all the response was positive. Laurence Gronlund, whose *Cooperative Commonwealth* had been replaced in *Twentieth Century*'s affections by *The Human Drift*, complained that Gillette's scheme was strikingly similar to one 'invented' by the Frenchman Charles Fourier 80 years before, noting with obvious distaste that Fourier had also been a commercial traveller. In a final swipe Gronlund wrote, 'I was surprised to find this book recommended as *sound* by a journal that ought to be on the intellectual summit of reform.'

Undaunted, the publishers of *Twentieth Century* went

on to produce a second edition of *The Human Drift*. In April the magazine changed its masthead motto from 'Hear the Other Side' to Gillette's 'United Intelligence and Material Equality'. An editorial announced that the newly formed Twentieth Century Company would soon offer shares to the public at $5 apiece – 'and we are happy to state that we have the hearty co-operation of the author, Mr King C Gillette, who will be the President of the Twentieth Century Company'.

In a subsequent issue the magazine offered 'a few words of introduction' to acquaint subscribers with the leader of the movement: 'He is of commanding appearance, standing fully six foot high, and would attract attention anywhere. A man of affairs, always accustomed to deal with large business interests, his success as a leader of an industrial movement would not be questioned by anyone who had ever met him.' The commercial traveller knew how to make a good first impression.

Not long afterwards the *New York World* treated its readers to a sarcastic account of 'Mr Gillette's wonderful plan to live in giant tenements', accompanied by a large illustration of one of Gillette's apartment houses. 'He thinks we should all be happy in these queer sky-parlours', it said, 'and that love in a cottage or a Fifth Avenue palace would no longer have any charms.' Describing his Metropolis as 'one big nation-city of happy idlers', the article dwelt on Gillette's claim that citizens need only work for five years. As far as the *World* was concerned, there were more pressing issues facing future Americans: the paper wanted to know whether Gillette's Metropolis would allow its saloons to sell beer on Sundays.

For all its flaws, though, Gillette's book struck a chord. Every week readers' letters to *Twentieth Century* proclaimed *The Human Drift* a revelation, its author a genius. They found his scheme refreshingly pragmatic – based squarely on 'present business methods' – and yet no one could say his ultimate goal wasn't radical enough.

For a few months Gillette wrote supportive articles for *Twentieth Century*, but in May he suddenly fell silent. Almost from the moment of its instigation, it seemed, he had lost interest in the project. In August the magazine apologised for the delay in publishing the company's prospectus, saying it was 'now in the hands of our president, Mr Gilette [sic], who will in his own admirable style put a finish and a tone to it which will convince all reasonable-minded persons that the control of production and distribution can safely be placed in the hands of the people'. October brought word that 'personal matters have occupied the attention of Mr Gillette, our president, to the exclusion of everything else'. But what were the 'personal matters' occupying Gillette? What could be more important than saving the world?

***

On a spring morning in 1895, with the public launch of the Twentieth Century Company in the offing, Gillette found himself alone with his thoughts – and his Star safety razor – in front of the bathroom mirror. He would later recall that by this time he had already moved to Marion Terrace in the western suburb of Brookline, although the *Boston Directory* for 1895 still lists him as living at 64 Westland Ave, in the Back Bay section of the city, in view of the just completed Christian Science Church. Wherever he was, he was by himself – his wife and four-year-old son were away visiting relatives in Ohio while the boy recovered from a minor throat operation.

In the grand scheme of things the Star razor, patented by Otto and Frederick Kampfe of Brooklyn in 1880, represented a relatively minor innovation in self-shaving. The 'safety razor', at least in name, had been conceived by a Frenchman, Jean-Jacques Perret, a century before. His version consisted of a straight razor partially embedded in a wooden guard that protected the user against more serious mishaps. Although Perret's razor was manufactured, it did not endure; even in the late 19th century the straight razor – with its naked blade – remained standard equipment. And yet, while it was well suited for use by a barber working on someone else's face, shaving oneself in a mirror with a straight razor was an awkward business, requiring great skill and patience. The most practised of users would allow half an hour for the procedure. Cuts and nicks were common badges of honour for self-shavers, especially young men who were still learning the art.

In 1847 an Englishman named William Henson had attempted to improve things by designing a razor with the blade set perpendicular to the handle, in the manner of a hoe. The Star safety razor (such as Gillette used) was one of these 'hoe-type' razors, with an elaborately decorated head and a patented wire guard to protect the user's face from nicks. But, if blood loss was greatly reduced by this safety razor, it was still pretty basic, and the problem of keeping the blade keen remained. Like straight razors, the stubby Star blades were made of forged steel and required stropping before each use. Eventually they would have to be professionally re-sharpened, and spare blades cost as much as $1.50 apiece. A man who had not planned carefully for such contingencies could well find himself with no recourse but to arrive at work unshaven, or to visit the barber on his way.

Appropriately enough, King Gillette was in precisely this predicament on that spring morning in 1895. 'I found my razor dull', he would write later, 'and not only was it dull but it was beyond the point of successful stropping and it needed honing, for which it must be taken to a barber or a cutler. As I stood there with the razor in my hand, my eyes resting on it as lightly as a bird settling down on its nest – the Gillette razor was born.'

Gillette had been searching for something to invent for some time. His father and elder brother had recently gone into business as the Gillette Clipping Machine Company, making power-driven horse clippers of their own design. His brother George had continued to patent other inventions ranging from bottle stoppers to 'swimming attachments'. Even his brother-in-law Charles Gaines had filed a patent the previous year for a 'conduit system for electrical railways'. The inventor who inspired Gillette most, though, was his employer William Painter, whose crown cork had been such a success that the Baltimore Bottle Seal Company had now changed its name to Crown Cork & Seal, as it is still known today. The simplicity and cost-effectiveness of the disposable tin cap was part of the sales pitch Gillette gave to brewers and bottlers up and down the East Coast. Obsessed with finding a similar invention, he had begun to run through the alphabet on train journeys, cataloguing every conceivable article to which disposability might apply.

He later described the moment of his enlightenment with all the poetic fancy of a patent application: 'At that time, and in that moment, it seemed as though I could see the way the blade could be held in a holder; then came the idea of sharpening the two opposite edges on a thin piece of steel that was uniform in thickness throughout, thus doubling its service; and following, in sequence, came the clamping plates for the blade with a handle equally disposed between the two edges of the blade.'

What Gillette had invented in his head was not so much a new kind of razor as a new kind of blade. A curved clamp would hold the blade steady, at the ideal angle, atop a hoe-type handle. But the blade would be wafer-thin, flexible, mass-produced, stamped from inexpensive sheet steel and sharpened to a keen edge on both sides. When one side became dull, the user would turn the razor round and shave with the other. When that side became dull, he would throw the blade away. Gillette had at last found his own bottle cap: a disposable product that created its own market. 'I have got it,' he wrote triumphantly to his wife. 'Our fortune is made.'

According to his own recollection, Gillette walked into Wilkinson's hardware store on Union Avenue that same day – presumably unshaven – and purchased a quantity of the steel ribbon used for clock springs from which to cut his first blades. In fact a full six months would elapse between the bathroom-sink epiphany and the first crude prototype. His initial inspiration had come to him, he said, 'as though the razor were already a finished thing and held before my eyes'. This proved to be even more of an illusion than he knew. It would be a further seven years before the razor finally existed.

The first hurdle was simply to explain the concept. Friends, family and bottle-cap customers scratched their heads as they listened to his idea and looked at his drawings. One asked to see a model. Gillette duly whittled one from a scrap of wood, but nothing about his descriptions or his little wooden carving inspired confidence or enthusiasm.

Nor was there any guarantee that the consumer would appreciate such an advance. The Gillette safety razor may have represented a revolution in shaving, but the concept of disposability was still in its infancy, and was always likely to meet with a certain amount of resistance. Even at the turn of the century, most men who shaved themselves were still using a straight razor, a product designed to last a lifetime or longer with proper care.

The real target was the barber-shop. Vast numbers of men were still shaved by the neighborhood barber, the majority of them submitting but twice a week, generally on Wednesdays and Saturdays. Photographs dating from that time, for which men obviously wanted to look their best, are misleading. A certain level of scruffiness prevailed, and was tolerated. Indeed, many men did not shave at all. Full beards were still prevalent, if not exactly fashionable, and moustaches and side-whiskers abounded, to the extent that streetcar conductors carried transfer tickets printed with four faces – one bearded, one mustachioed, one with side whiskers and one with a moustache-and-whiskers combination. Punching a hole in the picture that most closely resembled the recipient was considered sufficient identification (clean-shaven men received an unpunched ticket).

Could something as simple as a new razor render this system obsolete? Obviously there was a potential market for anything that set a new standard for 'clean-shaven', but would men really want to shave every day, even if they could?

All new products and concepts must finally face the judgment of a fickle public, but Gillette's razor suffered from a more immediate problem. It didn't work. His first prototype, completed in October 1895, was unusable. For reasons which are not at all apparent, this non-working model none the less convinced Gillette that he was on the right track. A second version didn't work either, but Gillette was still not dissuaded.

The biggest problem, it turned out, was putting a sharp enough edge on a piece of sheet steel. Gillette couldn't do it, even by hand, and machinists he consulted told him it was impossible – sheet steel was simply too soft to hold an edge, and too flimsy to harden sufficiently. And, even if he managed to solve this problem, he would still need to adapt the process to mass production. All of this was beyond the limited skills of a tinkerer like Gillette. If he couldn't make his razor, he needed to find someone who could.

Gillette was never a man to put all his eggs in one basket, of course. Following the initial disappointment of his first prototype razor, he went to work on another invention with more obvious potential, a system for feeding crown bottle caps into a bottling machine. Perhaps as a way of showing her support for an invention that was neither a utopian pipe dream nor an unworkable razor, his long-suffering wife Alanta bore witness to the patent application. Her husband made in excess of $5,000 a year selling bottle caps, a very good living for a turn-of-the-century salesman, but he had saved nothing over the years, nor had he done anything to secure a less peripatetic profession. Alanta Gillette might well have hoped that the bottle-cap feeder would replace the razor in his affections, just as the razor had replaced the utopia.

Her hopes were to prove vain. Bar a brief and confused foray into *Realpolitik* during the 1896 presidential election – when Gillette and *Twentieth Century* came out in support of the Democratic candidate, the agrarian populist William Jennings Bryan – and the publication of a small pamphlet entitled *The Ballot Box* following Bryan's defeat, Gillette's razor remained his primary preoccupation. His efforts, unfortunately, bore little fruit. Indeed, Gillette's radical notions about disposability were beginning to look as naive as his politics. Originally, he had intended for each blade, sold for a penny, to be used just once, and he had supposed that he could make 500 blades from a pound – 16 cents' worth – of steel ribbon; but such poor quality steel was unsuitable for the job. If better steel was used, replacing blades would be prohibitively expensive. Of course Gillette had yet to manage even a single shave with one of his experimental, hand-sharpened prototypes. No matter what he tried, the thin steel would not take an edge. Engineers at the Massachusetts Institute of Technology had already told him he was wasting his time. While travelling for Crown Cork & Seal, Gillette consulted cutlers and machinists in several different cities, but he found no one who could make his razor for him, or offer the least encouragement: 'Those whom I went to or consulted invariably advised me to drop it... They told me I was throwing my money away.'

In the face of such frank rejection, Gillette's single-mindedness was beginning to look like obsession, his self-belief an idiotic delusion. The very qualities which had carried him this far in his quest – the patience, the stubbornness, the salesman's impermeable carapace – now seemed poised to destroy him. 'I didn't know enough to quit,' he admitted some years later. 'If I had been technically trained I would have quit, or probably would never have begun.'

In fact King Gillette knew better than his detractors. He was for the most part a plodding inventor, who had long pursued a sideline for which he showed considerably less aptitude than his brothers. But he knew his razor was the real thing, the best idea he would ever have, a genuine innovation which he had stumbled across down an unlit, untrammelled path of investigation. With hindsight, Gillette's story would become a parable of persistence rewarded, but in 1897 he was still a 42-year-old travelling salesman with a wife, a child and a misplaced confidence in an unworkable idea which consumed all his spare time and cash.

And he had little enough money to throw away. Only recently, with someone else financing him, he had branched out with another sideline venture, as a partner in a soft-drinks business called the New Era Carbonator Company ('New Era', a familiar utopian trope, was also the name of the publishing company of the first edition of *The Human Drift*). Gillette's backer lost $40,000 before he abandoned the project, leaving Gillette owing him nearly half that amount.

A prototype razor of sorts did finally come into being when Gillette persuaded an experienced German cutler named Franz to make some handles from his designs. For the most satisfactory of these Franz also made three double-edged blades, hardening and sharpening them as best he could. Using this model, King Gillette became the first man to shave himself with a disposable safety razor, but the result was far from ideal. He continued to tinker with the design for another year and a half, and in spite of Franz's help the blade problems persisted. At last, in the summer of 1899, with his invention in the best shape he could get it, he applied for a patent.

As the new century dawned, America's troubled conscience began to ease itself. Already much of the *fin-de-siècle* uncertainty of the preceding decade had been swept away. The vogue for utopian schemes had dissipated as economic prosperity had returned; *Twentieth Century* magazine had shut up shop two years before. On the strength of a buoyant Wall Street, William McKinley had recently won another term as President, beating William Jennings Bryan for a second time, by an even greater margin. For King Gillette, however, there was little cause for celebration. Indeed his 45th birthday – on 5 January 1900 – came merely as an unpleasant reminder of his age, and the fact that his razor was no more a commercial reality than when he had first conceived it five years before. Publicly he was as enthusiastic as ever, smiling when friends greeted him and chirpily asked after 'the razor' as if it were some long-standing minor ailment. But alone in front of his shaving mirror, his latest prototype in hand, he must sometimes have wished the inspiration had never visited him.

Not surprisingly, Gillette's efforts to attract investment were running aground. 'I approached many friends and strangers in an effort to secure capital,' he recalled, 'but when my prospective capitalists would blow cold, it gave me a chill, and I did not have the courage to press my point.' The prototype did, however, attract the attention of one of Gillette's friends, Edward Stewart, a bottler and crown cork customer who offered to show the razor round on Gillette's behalf.

One night at the house of a Brookline neighbour called Henry Sachs, Stewart handed the razor to an engineer and inventor named William Nickerson. Nickerson was not in the least impressed. The razor, he said, 'did not appeal to me as being a very practicable implement. The blade was rather stiff for the handle, which was of too light construction.' His initial reaction may have had something to do with the fact that Nickerson had always shaved himself with an old straight razor given to him by his father.

Nickerson was an intriguing case. After graduating from the Massachusetts Institute of Technology in 1876, he had launched himself on a varied and adventurous life of successful inventing and business failure. He had developed a new method of obtaining tannic acid from tree bark, spent six months dredging for gold in Georgia and a similar period operating a saw-mill, before returning to Boston broke and unemployed. Shortly after his return, he had read about an elevator crash that had killed several people, and he immediately set about inventing a number of safety devices, including the push-button floor-selector and the mechanism which prevents the lift doors from opening until the car arrives. Like King Gillette, he had consistently failed to make any money from his inventions, ingenious though they were. While working for the Beacon Vacuum Pump and Electrical Company, he had developed a radical new way of manufacturing light bulbs. He had gone on to invent several devices for the New England Weighing Machine Company. He was known by those who had worked with him as a prickly and private man, but also as someone who could solve the unsolvable. His dismissal of Gillette's razor should have been the kiss of death.

A year or so later Jacob Heilborn, a former partner of Nickerson in the Beacon Vacuum enterprise, asked Nickerson to look at the razor again. After being approached by Edward Stewart, Heilborn had seen commercial possibilities in Gillette's idea, and he was keen for Nickerson to apply his considerable skills to the problem. Again Nickerson refused. Finally Heilborn 'fairly begged' Nickerson to take on the razor and Nickerson reluctantly agreed to consider the project for a month.

On 9 September 1901, Nickerson wrote a letter to Heilborn, which represented something of an about-face. 'It is my confident opinion', he wrote, 'that not only can a successful razor be made on the principles of the Gillette patent, but that if the blades are made by proper methods a result in advance of anything known can be reached.' He proposed an initial budget of $5,000 and predicted that four months would be ample time to design and build the first machines for the manufacture of blades.

A few days after receiving the letter, an excited Jacob Heilborn called Gillette and Nickerson to his office on Exchange Street and introduced them for the first time. The mood at the meeting would have been oddly sombre: President McKinley had just died, a week after being shot twice in the stomach by an anarchist. Flags in the streets of Boston were at half-mast. Shop windows were dressed in black crepe, with portraits of the slain President on display. At such a time a celebration of the new partnership would have been unseemly, but there were other reasons for Gillette and Nickerson to be sparing with their enthusiasm.

Seventeen years after this meeting, Gillette and Nickerson each produced separate accounts of the development of the razor for the Gillette *Blade*, the company's in-house magazine. By that time both men had seen the wisdom of generously crediting the other for his part in the invention, although it is clear even from these accounts that things were a bit different in 1901. Nickerson felt that Gillette saw the making of the razor into a practical reality as a minor detail in comparison to its initial conception, and had no idea of the considerable difficulties which still lay ahead. Gillette felt that his razor – for so long a dream shared by no one – was now slipping from his control, and he was reluctant to leave its exploitation to others. Gillette and Nickerson claimed to have liked each other right away, but a certain underlying animosity had one immediate result. When their new company was incorporated a few weeks later according to the laws of the State of Maine, it was named, at William Nickerson's insistence, the American Safety Razor Company. 'I felt that I was going to play such a large part in the making of the razor,' said Nickerson, 'that it would be an injustice to me to name it after Mr Gillette.'

The company was incorporated with 50,000 ten-dollar shares. Gillette, Heilborn and Stewart were directors and Gillette was president. To raise the $5,000 needed by Nickerson, the directors decided to sell 20 blocks of 500 shares for the knockdown price of $250 per block. Ten thousand shares remained in the treasury, while Stewart,

Heilborn and Nickerson divided up 12,500 shares for themselves, leaving Gillette with 17,500.

Nickerson set to work in a friend's machine shop at 394 Atlantic Avenue. The first order of business was to design a new handle. Gillette's model had been fashioned from sheet metal, and the result was light and flimsy. Nickerson quickly realised that in order for it to provide the thin, flexible blade with the necessary rigidity, the handle itself would need to be far more substantial and machined out of solid steel. Next he redesigned the shape of the blade, slicing a rectangle out of a circle one-and-three-quarter inches in diameter, to create a blade with rounded sides and a cutting edge an inch-and-a-half long. He then had to design machines to harden and sharpen the blades.

Steel is hardened by a process of heating and cooling, usually with a forge or furnace and with water, but such extremes of temperature wreaked havoc on sheet steel just 6,000th of an inch thick. Even when tightly stacked in a specially designed press, the hot steel blades would buckle and bend beyond salvaging. Nickerson first tried to keep the blades flat by interleaving them with iron plates, but the plates buckled as well. Then he tried perforating each blade with an odd pattern designed to relieve the lateral stresses. This didn't work either, and by now his first sharpening machine was completed. Eventually after further experimentation Nickerson came up with a solution. The blades were interleaved with sheets of copper, which conducted the heat away rapidly, ensuring that the stack cooled at a uniform rate. The process was, in its first incarnation, ridiculously laborious, but it worked.

The sharpening process was carried out on an 'abrading machine', a complex, belt-driven merry-go-round of stone grinding wheels which slowly but automatically put an edge on the hardened blades. By the summer of 1902, the best samples from Nickerson's halting little assembly-line were a cause for unaccustomed optimism among the company's directors. Gillette seized the moment and called a special meeting of stockholders on 15 July, where he succeeded in having the corporation rechristened the Gillette Safety Razor Company.

The directors' optimism proved to be premature. There may have been light at the end of the tunnel, but the train was now stalled on the tracks. The company had long since used up its initial $5,000, and was now several thousand dollars in debt. Employees hired by Nickerson had gone for weeks without pay. The company attempted to raise revenue by selling the remaining shares in the treasury, but there were no takers. Several early investors who had never taken the razor seriously had already sold out for what they could get. Shares which had originally been discounted at 50 cents each were now changing hands privately for half that amount. By September, a few weeks shy of the company's first anniversary, receivership looked inevitable. After a particularly depressing directors' meeting, Gillette walked to Young's restaurant, a frequent haunt of his, where he met an old friend – John Joyce.

It is unlikely that Gillette's encounter with Joyce that afternoon was by chance. Both men regularly took lunch at Young's, and by Gillette's own admission he and Joyce had dined together there 'hundreds and hundreds of times, in fact nearly every day for years'. It is probable that Gillette went looking for Joyce, knowing that the wealthy Irish brewery owner was his last hope. It was also likely that Joyce knew of Gillette's predicament already. In many ways Joyce was the perfect candidate to bail out the ailing razor company: he was rich, a personal friend of Gillette, and he had been particularly impressed with the sample razor Gillette had recently given him, along with a gift of 1,250 shares of stock. In fact there was only one reason why Gillette had avoided approaching him sooner. Joyce was the man who had backed Gillette in the failed New Era Carbonator Company, and Gillette already owed him $19,700. Under these circumstances, the conversation was probably at least as stilted as Gillette's recollection.

'King, what's the matter?' asked Joyce. 'You look worried.'

'I am worried,' replied Gillette. 'And thoroughly discouraged. We have had a meeting of the razor company this morning and we are at the end of our rope.' Joyce did not let Gillette play-act for too long. He agreed to bail out the razor company in return for an issue of $100,000-worth of bonds bearing eight per cent interest, plus an equal amount of stock, although he would put up the money only as it was needed to run the operation and reserved the right to pull out once he had paid in $30,000. It was a hard bargain, but Gillette had few other options.

In a matter of days Joyce's money was flowing into the company's accounts. Gillette, however, felt uneasy. While extremely naive about business – he already appeared to be out of his depth – he knew enough to know that with each injection of outside capital he was relinquishing control over his invention. Already there were directors to answer to, and stockholders to reassure. Heilborn and Nickerson, with their longstanding working relationship, sometimes seemed to regard his input as an intrusion. Now the hard-nosed John Joyce, a man whose success was owed to an overriding concern for the bottom line, held a majority stake in Gillette's dream.

At the beginning of 1903 William Nickerson moved the production operation to larger quarters, taking over the top floor of 394 Atlantic Avenue, and began to tool up for large-scale manufacture. Having worked in relative isolation for a year, he now came under tremendous pressure to produce results quickly and cheaply, from Joyce in particular, but also from Gillette, who simply couldn't afford to lose any more of Joyce's money. But Gillette was often away on bottle-cap business, and, it seems, disengaged enough from the day-to-day development of the razor to find time to work on other inventions: in January he filed a patent application for a bottle-labelling machine. It was Nickerson who now felt trapped 'between the upper and nether millstones', as he confessed later. The sample razors he had lovingly produced may have been satisfactory, but turning them out in sufficient quantity and sufficiently cheaply meant overcoming huge technical obstacles which still remained.

John Joyce, now a member of the board of directors, insisted on setting the price of a razor set – a handle and 20 blades – at $5, two dollars more than the other directors considered appropriate, and twice the price of a decent imported straight razor. A Chicago firm called Townsend & Hunt was engaged to market the razor, initially by mail order. In October 1903 the first advert for the Gillette razor appeared in *System* magazine, and later that month the first razors and blades were packed into their white pasteboard boxes and shipped to customers. By the end of the year the company had sold a grand total of 51 razor sets.

The following year looked to be promising for the

Gillette Safety Razor Company, if not for King Gillette. Although he was president of the company he drew no salary, and he was still working full-time selling bottle caps. In the autumn of 1903 Crown Cork & Seal had assigned him a new territory: London. Not wishing to leave at this critical juncture, Gillette asked the directors of the razor company to provide him with an income so that he might quit his day job, but they refused. On 9 January 1904, therefore, King Gillette reluctantly resigned as president, leaving his old friend Ward Holloway, the man who had once helped him finance the publication of *The Human Drift*, in his place. Later that month he left Boston for New York, and set sail for Europe.

From the deck of the steamship *Cedric*, King Gillette watched the New York skyline fade in the pale winter light. He did not know when he would see America again; his new London job was an indefinite posting. Accompanied by his wife, his 13-year-old son and an assistant in the person of his brother-in-law Charles Gaines, he had boarded with all his worldly possessions, including a healthy supply of his newfangled razors. Under different circumstances Gillette might have been happy to be leaving – the transfer came with a substantial pay rise, and he was no stranger to England, where he had sold Sapolio 15 years before – but as New York resolved itself into the horizon, it is difficult to imagine his thoughts being on anything but the fledgling razor company he had left behind, which now seemed destined to succeed – or perish – without him.

By all accounts Gillette missed a troubled period in the company's history. Although the razor sets were beginning to sell well, it was still costing them too much to manufacture blades, about five cents each for labour alone, while they were selling packs of 20 blades for a dollar. Persistent manufacturing problems meant that Nickerson could not cope with demand, and funds were urgently needed to scale up production and increase efficiency. When Joyce's final promised cash injection failed to cover monthly expenses, a previously rejected proposal (by Joyce) to sell the foreign rights to manufacture Gillette razors was reconsidered.

Gillette was keeping himself busy during his exile – he personally founded the razor company's English branch, which operated out of Crown Cork & Seal's offices near City Road, in London – but he was furious when word reached him of developments back in Boston. He had always argued passionately against selling the foreign rights to his razor. In August, with his entire future at stake, he left his brother-in-law in charge of both the bottle caps and the razor blades and hurried to Liverpool to book a passage to America. He did not make it to Boston for the meeting on the 29th at which Nickerson,

Joyce and Holloway finally agreed to relinquish the foreign rights, but he soon found a way to reverse the decision. How is unclear. Gillette recalled only that he 'protested against the proposed disposition of our foreign rights and won my point, and in view of the fact that the company was making money rapidly I insisted on a salaried position, which was agreed to'. Nickerson's recollection is even more vague. He said simply that 'Mr Gillette suddenly returned from Europe and not finding things to his liking began taking an active part in the management of the company.' Against the intractable Joyce, an emotional appeal may have been Gillette's best weapon. No doubt some who disagreed with the inventor's position found it difficult to do so face to face.

Even Gillette must have been surprised at the abrupt way in which his long-held dreams of success had been realised. At last he was able to go to Baltimore and resign his position at Crown Cork & Seal. The directors at Crown Cork listened with growing interest as Gillette jubilantly explained the reason for his resignation, and before he departed they persuaded him to part with 4,000 of his remaining 9,000 shares for the startling sum of $80,000, more than he had earned in his 13 years selling bottle caps. He returned to Boston with a cheque for half that amount in his pocket. In a typically awkward attempt to capture the moment he later remarked: 'If the road between Baltimore and Boston had been paved with eggs and I had been obliged to walk the whole distance, I would not have broken an egg.' He used some of the money to replenish his holdings in the company, but the first thing Gillette did when he reached Boston was to write out a cheque to John Joyce for the sum of $19,700, the amount he owed him from the collapse of the New Era Carbonator Company.

If this transaction ended an awkward obligation between the two directors, it also represented a formal end to Gillette's and Joyce's friendship. The dispute over the foreign rights to the razor had opened a rift between the two which threatened the stability of the new company, so much so that a panicky William Nickerson was moved to sell a large chunk of his stock. According to Nickerson the 'contention' which developed between Gillette and Joyce 'lasted till the beginning of the year 1912'. But that was eight years away, and things were going to get a lot worse before they got better.

***

A few months after his return, Gillette was made vice-president of the company that bore his name, with John Joyce as president. Confident of his position perhaps for the first time, he then set sail for London to retrieve his family. While he was away, on 15 November 1904, the US

Patent Office finally granted him patent no 775,134, which began, 'Be it known that I King C Gillette, a citizen of the United States, residing at Brookline, in the county of Norfolk and State of Massachusetts, have invented certain new and useful Improvements in Razors.'

This fact would soon become widely known indeed. By the spring of 1905 the production problems that had plagued the company the previous year were largely solved and Nickerson's crew was moving into a new factory in south Boston. Advertising began in earnest, with the razor's inventor very much at the centre of the campaign. Former shareholders in the bygone Twentieth Century Company must have been bemused, to say the least. The kindly face that had once featured in advertisements for *The Human Drift* under the banner of 'United Intelligence and Material Equality', was now being used to sell razor blades alongside the two-handed slogan 'No Stropping, No Honing'. In 1906 blade sales overtook razor sales for the first time, and in the single year 1908 1.2 million packets of Gillette blades were purchased, each bearing the likeness and signature of their inventor, King C Gillette.

Gillette's boardroom battles with John Joyce, the biggest shareholder, continued. While Gillette felt that Joyce had little vision beyond his own pecuniary interests, Joyce knew enough of Gillette to realise he was capable of being financially reckless. Gillette had already shifted some of the company's ancillary manufacturing operations to Newark, New Jersey, and had plans to expand there, a move which Joyce regarded as a pointless expense. But Joyce may have been even more disturbed to find that the company's figurehead and trademark had recently also returned to his first love.

In July 1906 *National Magazine* carried an article titled 'World Corporation (Unlimited)' by King C Gillette, a synopsis 'in anticipation of the more extended and detailed prospectus which is shortly to appear'. World Corporation was an updated version of the plan Gillette had first set out in *The Human Drift*, but the refinements were largely technical. Gillette was now advocating a network of banks in which shareholders would deposit their dollars. The resulting wealth would be used to purchase securities in other corporations. He illustrates his scheme most clearly by example: 'John Jones owns a thousand shares of Pennsylvania railroad stock. He concludes that World Corporation shares are a safer investment, and he therefore sells his Pennsylvania shares in the open market, takes his money and deposits it in the World Corporation Bank in the city or town where he lives, each dollar representing a share ownership. The World Corporation Board of Finance now has his money to invest, and may possibly purchase the thousand shares of Pennsylvania given up by John Jones. Thereafter those shares have disappeared from the stock market forever. This process of conversion continues throughout the whole world daily until every material asset of the world worth purchasing is made an asset of World Corporation.'

Once again Gillette's confidence in the system is unassailable. 'One of the most singular things in connection with this enterprise', he writes, 'is the impossibility of its failure.' However, one detail of his plan is noticeably absent: there is no mention of a giant Metropolis of 25-storey skyscrapers on the banks of Lake Ontario. Gillette must have realised how dated this once daring vision would seem to his readers. The world had changed a great deal in the 12 years since the publication of *The Human Drift*. The telephone and the automobile were now commonplace, if not exactly universal. In 1903 Orville and Wilbur Wright had managed the first 12-second flight in their crude aeroplane. The Flatiron building in New York had been completed in 1902, and at 20 storeys was the world's tallest building. Even Gillette's dream of obtaining electricity from Niagara Falls had been realised a decade before. Set against the present, Gillette's futuristic Metropolis was beginning to look distinctly quaint.

Alongside the article in *National Magazine*, a brief sketch of the utopian razor baron is offered by the editor, who had recently met Gillette and had been instantly won over: 'He is tall… with a kindly smile and generous impulses which win for him the good will of all who come into personal contact with him.'

His impression of Gillette is remarkably similar to the one recorded by the editor of *Twentieth Century* 12 years before. Both men seem to have fallen under Gillette's spell, his salesman's talent for radiating warmth. Undoubtedly, in person Gillette could be extremely persuasive. Even his rivals in the razor company could not contend with his presence in the boardroom. He had always possessed what the Old Drummer's pamphlet called the 'essential virtue of self-abnegation': while he would never knowingly admit to acting in his own best interests, he rarely came out of a meeting without getting what he wanted.

He could not, however, enlist subscribers to his World Corporation one at a time, and his convoluted prose was a poor substitute for the salesman's accomplished soft sell. His impact on the editor notwithstanding, a planned further article for *National Magazine* on the subject of World Corporation never materialised. When his picture next appeared in those pages four months later, it was part of a full-page advertisement for his other invention. 'Just a Gillette Safety Razor, soap and brush…' read the copy, 'and in 2 to 5 minutes the harshest beard can be smoothly shaved from the tenderest skin.'

Gillette did, however, have a broader examination of

his World Corporation in the works. In a letter to the editor of *National Magazine*, he announced that, 'A complete presentment of my plan is now being prepared by Mr Melvin L Severy of Arlington Heights.' He gave away little beyond the title, *Gillette's Social Redemption*: 'It is impossible to give you a comprehensive idea of this work in a letter. Suffice to say that it represents all my years of thought and study on the subject.'

Even in the broad pool of Gillette's acquaintance, Melvin Severy was an odd fish. Pale, balding and eight years younger than Gillette, Severy was an even more dedicated filer of patent applications, as many as five or six a year. By 1906 he had nearly 30 patents to his name.

When King Gillette was first formulating his World Corporation plan in a Pennsylvania hotel room, Melvin Severy was the 26-year-old editor of the *Esoteric*, a creepy Boston monthly concerned with, among other things, hygiene, theosophy, practical occultism and 'solar biology', ie astrology. For a time he ran his own printing company, employing the 'Severy Process', and he later invented the choralcelo, an electromagnetic keyboard instrument that took up several rooms when fully installed, and of which only six were ever sold. Most recently he had taken up writing thrillers, and somewhere along the way had become a convert to Gillette's cause. Gillette hoped the writer could make a more persuasive case for World Corporation than he had been able to do (one wonders if Gillette had read the review in *Outlook* of Severy's most recent thriller, which called it 'a tissue of preposterous absurdities, and, moreover, an exceedingly badly written book').

The first instalment of Severy's version of Gillette's 'complete presentment' appeared in 1907. Weighing in at 783 pages, *Gillette's Social Redemption* contains next to nothing about Gillette's ideas, although there is a photograph of the 'inventor of the system', the same likeness, taken by Benjamin Falk in 1906, that would grace tens of billions of packets of razor blades over 60 years. Beginning with the fateful words, 'This book is not intended to be interesting,' Severy sets out to convince readers of the need for reform by cataloguing injustice on a global scale, including recent outrages perpetrated in the Congo, poverty in Russia, railroad negligence and New York slum conditions. 'It may be that some of the world's scandals are omitted from this large and handsome book, of whose paper and print it is possible to speak well,' read the catty *New York Times* review, which declined to pass judgment on Gillette's 'system' on the scant information available: 'Although the authors are unable to communicate their ideas, they give us their portraits. They are nice-looking gentlemen, whose features scarcely reflect the age, labor and care which accompany deep thought.'

A full description of 'the ingenious plan which Mr Gillette has devised' was reserved for another book, the 598-page *Gillette's Industrial Solution*, which disappointingly picked up where the previous tome left off. It featured a photograph of Gillette in a fetching straw hat over a caption that read: 'The argument most frequently used against Socialism is that its sponsors are dreamers... or those whose failure in life has made them dissatisfied with present conditions. As a successful inventor and head of one of the largest corporations in the world, King C Gillette is an eloquent refutation of this theory.'

Although Severy's two-volume explication of Gillette's 'industrial solution' made a brave attempt to tie the scheme to contemporary reform movements, it was at best a further muddling of Gillette's confused utopianism. Gillette himself, however, seemed pleased enough with the result. He paid for the private publication of both books and sent scores of signed copies to public libraries, where many still languish undisturbed.

In the meantime, Gillette was more than living up to Severy's assessment of him as a hard-headed businessman. In 1906 he formed a holding company to consolidate his stock with that held by his family and friends, in an attempt to create a majority voting block in the razor company and oust John Joyce from the president's chair. In what was many years later related as an amusing anecdote, Gillette arranged to purchase some shares held by one Charles Flaccus, a Pittsburgh bottle manufacturer who had bought a $250 block of the original stock in the hope that the gesture would bring him some extra bottle business. Mr Flaccus had then returned home, put the certificates in his safe and forgotten all about them. Just four years later Gillette had to borrow money to buy them back. They were worth $62,500. With these additional shares Gillette now effectively controlled the razor company, and by January 1908 the inventor and founder had manoeuvred his way back into the presidency, a post he had not held for four years.

Gillette's triumphant return to the helm was not greeted with unalloyed enthusiasm by the board of directors. His plans were often grandiose, expensive and, like the very razor idea on which the company was founded, seemingly unworkable. A 1951 study of the development of the Gillette razor quoted an anonymous associate from the early days who remarked that Gillette 'could wreck a company as well as he could build one'. Along with his long-term plan to move operations to Newark, he came up with a radical scheme to manufacture blades continuously out of spools of steel ribbon (a process which, to his credit, eventually prevailed) and he inaugurated a doomed attempt to expand the company's operations into steel production. The essential question was one of money.

Joyce and others felt the funds for Gillette's schemes would be better shared out as dividends among the directors. Gillette wrote bitterly of these board-room enemies: 'They think everything is right that is done within the law; to them business is business, and when the dollar glitters, friendship and moral right can go to the devil. Such are the type of some around me now. They are not honest and they are dangerous.'

Of course, King Gillette himself could be said to have sold out his own utopian principles. The man who had railed against the great Satan of competition and its attendant devils – advertising, the legal profession and production for profit – had become a renowned business leader in the very system he despised. His company was well-known for its pioneering use of advertising; his own likeness acted as a trademark in countless ads and on millions of packets of blades (the green wrapper, with Gillette's face at the centre, was modelled on the dollar bill). Gillette himself travelled daily to his presidential office in Boston from a fine house in the grand suburb of Brookline, the birthplace of that bastion of modern American privilege, the country club. The admiring editor of *National Magazine* had described Gillette as a man with 'a devotion to his life work that has kept him from ever belonging to clubs or attending banquets', but he was nonetheless a model capitalist. Like an evangelist in a gold suit, Gillette could at the very least be accused of failing to practise what he preached.

Gillette rarely addressed himself to this contradiction, and never directly. His most explicit justification went thus: 'The man who, under our present system, did not invest his capital to yield him a secure and comfortable income would be a fool indeed. The management that did not operate its business so as to yield large dividends would only lose what capital it had, and if anyone was the gainer, it would be some rival concern, not humanity as a whole.' Such reasoning was undoubtedly easier to accept from a humble bottle-cap salesman than the president of a large manufacturing concern, but if Gillette could not amalgamate the two worlds he inhabited, he appeared to have no trouble switching between them. When he wore his reforming hat, Gillette would not hesitate to criticise his fellow plutocrats ('The only difference between a Republic and a Monarchy is that we do not call our idle rich Kings Dukes and Princes'), without even recognising the irony. The success of his razor and the failure of his utopia were both the result of the same strange flaw: when King Gillette believed he was right, he was only too capable of ignoring the obvious.

In 1910 John Joyce filed a suit against Gillette and his holding company, in an effort to restrict voting rights to individual shareholders. For a time the litigation (which coincided with the costly defence of several patent infringement suits) threatened to destroy the ten-year-old Gillette Safety Razor Company. Then, after several years of fruitless wrangling, Joyce tried another tack: he offered to buy Gillette and his allies out, at the handsome price of $87.50 a share. King Gillette, weary of the boardroom feuding and thoroughly disillusioned by his tenure as president, accepted. The man who as a young inventor had always believed in – as he put it – the 'gold at the foot of the rainbow promise' finally received a bittersweet reward for his years of unrequited self-belief: almost $1 million for about two-thirds of his stock. Joyce once again became the majority shareholder. Gillette retained his salary and the title of president, but he gradually began to drift away from the day-to-day affairs of the company, and towards permanent residence in California.

***

During the stormiest period of his presidency in 1910, with both internal and external litigation pending, King Gillette had one other thing on his mind: he had a new book out, and this one, *World Corporation*, was written by Gillette himself. A statement at the beginning of the book, 'written at the request of Mr Severy', declares that *World Corporation* 'should be read as a self-contained proposition, separate and apart from any previous writings, and as exhibiting Mr Gillette's individual views and final conclusions', leaving it uncertain as to who was the more injured party in the dissolution of the Gillette-Severy partnership. Gillette had clearly decided to take matters into his own hands in more ways than one, for his 'World Corporation' had already been set up. A facsimile of the Articles of Incorporation, filed on 8 June 1910 in the Territory of Arizona, graces the opening pages.

World Corporation had its headquarters not in Phoenix, but at 6 Beacon Street, Boston, the offices of Edward S Crockett, Gillette's attorney as well as vice-president of the new corporation. Gillette was president and treasurer, with his brother-in-law Charles Gaines, who was also now the general manager of the razor factory, rounding out the board of directors. Incorporating his company under the liberal laws of the western territory (Arizona did not become a state until 1912) allowed Gillette to write a charter without any capital limitations. Like the United Company before it, World Corporation's capitalisation would be 'progressive and unlimited', expanding as the wealth of the world flowed into its coffers. Shares were a dollar each, and would be redeemed only at par value.

The book was, in effect, a prospectus for the newly incorporated organisation, but the basic ideas found in *The Human Drift* had changed little, as Gillette seemed content merely to fine-tune a system he had considered unassailable from the first. There is a certain sense of urgency in the book – Gillette wasn't getting any younger – which is most obviously manifested in his liberal use of the upper case. 'THE DISEASE WHICH SOONER OR LATER REACHES THE HEART AND BRAIN OF A NATION AND DESTROYS IT,' he writes, 'IS INDIVIDUALISM.' Fifteen years after he had first committed his ideas to print, Gillette was, if nothing else, still a master of the bloated epigram.

Such interest as *World Corporation* did receive was prompted by the fact that Gillette offered Teddy Roosevelt $1 million to serve as its president for four years, or rather he offered to be the first of 20 men to offer Roosevelt $50,000 towards that end. For publicity's sake, Gillette could hardly have made a better choice. Roosevelt had effectively retired as US President the previous year, refusing to seek a third term of office, but he remained the most popular politician in America and many suspected (rightly, as it turned out) that he would challenge his hand-picked successor, William Howard Taft, for the Republican nomination in 1912. 'WANTS ROOSEVELT TO HEAD HIS TRUST' read the headline in the *New York Times*, above an article which uncharitably compared Gillette's plan for World Corporation to 'the snake which defeated starvation by swallowing its own tail'. Sadly for Gillette (and for Taft), Roosevelt did not take up the offer, but then neither did the 19 other capitalists who were meant to provide the rest of Colonel Roosevelt's salary.

Even in 1894 Gillette's ideas had sat uneasily enough alongside conventional politics, but now he was profoundly out of step with the times. In the intervening 16 years progressive reform had become mainstream, pushing radical and revolutionary thinking to the furthest fringes of politics. Ironically it was Teddy Roosevelt who had ushered in this age of reform, curbing the power of the most abusive trusts, regulating the railroads and initiating basic health legislation. Taft continued the work, authorising the collection of federal income tax for the first time. Capitalism – 'competition for material wealth', as Gillette called it – was being incrementally tamed, and therefore enshrined.

Not that conventional politics mattered to a man who, sitting at his desk in his Brookline mansion or his presidential office, wrote of doing away with all nations and governments, along with 50,000 cities and towns and seven million farms in pursuit of a collectivist corporate paradise. 'I would rather work for a "World Corporate System"', he wrote, 'than be a large proprietor or capitalist under a competitive system, or a large stockholder in any individual corporation.' He was of course both, and with his own company riven by feuding and litigation, it is easy to imagine the publicity brought by World

Corporation was hardly welcomed by John Joyce, who had long tolerated Gillette's weird sideline as a utopian. The publicity itself achieved little. World Corporation never achieved the first 5,000 subscribers which Gillette wanted before he launched *World Corporation News*. The whole business passed quietly into non-existence.

***

With the founder parcelled off and the internal feuding at an end, the Gillette Safety Razor Company's profits increased steadily. The company's south Boston factory site was expanded, and in 1914 William Nickerson, the inventive genius who was still very much the technical expert at the centre of the Gillette operation, designed fully-automated systems to replace his old merry-go-round machines. As the United States prepared to enter the war raging in Europe, Gillette sent a message to the annual sales convention in which he said, 'in bearing our share of the financial burden made necessary by the tragedy of war we must not complain but do our part willingly'. The Gillette company's part, as it happened, was to provide each serviceman with a field razor set, with Uncle Sam footing the bill. In 1918 the corporation sold 3.5 million razors to the US military alone.

In retirement King Gillette had become a very rich man, and he began to spend money prodigiously on various different projects. In Tulare County in California he established a large orange grove, some of the yield of which was crated up and sent to employees of the Boston factory at Christmas. In 1917, Gillette and two partners purchased an eight-acre gold-mining claim in Colorado's San Juan mountains. Gillette also took a liking to Palm Springs – a burgeoning desert resort 120 kilometres east of Los Angeles. In nearby Indio he became a partner in a date ranch, 108 acres of date palms grown from offshoots specially imported from the Far East. And he bought and built several big homes in and around Los Angeles, as incautious acquisition gave way to sheer extravagance. One such purchase was a house on Ocean Boulevard in Santa Monica which, when he sold it in 1921, became the 40-room Hotel Miramar.

When the Gillette company director Henry J Fuller travelled to California in 1925, he paid a visit to Gillette at his home in Beverly Hills. Noting that Gillette had recently turned 70, he wrote, 'I was therefore surprised to find that at the present time he is engaged in building three homes for himself.' One of the houses was in Hollywood, another in the Tahquitz Estates in Palm Springs, near his date ranch, and the third at Balboa, on Newport harbour, just south of Los Angeles.

Big houses suited Gillette, for he had taken a large part of his family west with him. When his father died in 1903, just as the razor was getting off the ground, Gillette's mother had quit New York and come to live in Brookline. Now she came to live with him and his wife in Los Angeles. Eventually his mother-in-law, his siblings (Fanny died in Los Angeles in 1912, as did George three years later), his brother-in-law Charles and his grown son 'Kingie' all came to California, too.

As the only really successful member of his family, Gillette became a generous scion, but the constant presence of his relations inevitably became an irritant: 'In Cal. there is always too much family,' he wrote, 'and one has little time to really live their own life. To me it is a terrible thing for anyone to live the lives of other people and neglect their own desires and interests and things they want to do. And usually these other people have nothing to do themselves and only expect to be amused. It kills me to put myself in such a life day after day – so I prefer to travel.' Having constructed an elaborate retirement paradise for himself, Gillette now stayed away for many months at a time.

The war prevented him from going far at first – in 1918 the only foreign country he visited was Canada, on a tour of the Gillette factory in Montreal – but after the Armistice Gillette was free to wander. In 1922 he spent nearly a year visiting Britain, France, Switzerland, Spain, Portugal, Italy and northern Africa, dropping in on

Gillette representatives as he went. In an article about the trip for the Gillette *Blade* accompanied by photographs – one is simply captioned 'Native beggar types' – the voluble company president described being stranded for five days with his wife and a friend in the desert town of Touggout. 'While waiting we went to a little store to purchase some food in sealed packages or tins to supplement our Arab fare. I noticed on a show case in this store several Gillette razors and some cartons of blades.' Wherever he went he was recognised, and treated like a celebrity. Thanks to millions of little labels his name and face were, like his razor blades, 'Known the world over'.

Retirement did not stifle Gillette's interest in either invention or business, although as a multimillionaire his approach was somewhat different. To satisfy a new-found interest in automobiles and their components (he now had three chauffeur-driven Pierce Arrow limousines), Gillette hired the inventor Benjamin Schmidt, whose new patents for transmission mechanisms were assigned to the Gillette-Schmidt Gear Shift Company. Schmidt also patented several pieces of oil-well drilling equipment, with half the rights split between King C Gillette and his son Kingie. Gillette himself headed the Goldenwest Petroleum Company, operating oil wells in central California, and became president of the Gore Oil Company when that company subsumed Goldenwest in 1926.

So busy was he with travel, agriculture, real estate deals, business propositions, oil drilling, occasional trips to the Boston factory or inspirational articles for the *Blade*, it would be no wonder if King Camp Gillette had long forgotten about his dreams for a corporate utopia. But he hadn't. In fact he had been planning another assault on the public imagination for some time.

***

Soon after the war, Gillette paid a visit to the muckraking writer Upton Sinclair, whose 1906 book *The Jungle* had exposed the squalid conditions in Chicago's meat-packing industry, provoking an outcry which had in turn prompted Teddy Roosevelt to introduce the Pure Food and Drug Act and the Meat Inspection Act. Easing his huge frame into the back of one of his limousines, Gillette instructed his chauffeur to take him to Sinclair's modest home in Pasadena and, having been told by a secretary that Sinclair was not to be disturbed while working, presented his business card wrapped in a $100 bill.

Sinclair said it was unclear whether the banknote was meant for him or his secretary (he also neglects to mention who ended up with it), but the ploy certainly got his attention. Despite the awkward beginning to their acquaintance, it is clear that Sinclair took an immediate liking to the 'razor king', as he called him. In his autobiography Sinclair gave his first impression of Gillette: 'He was a large gentleman with white hair and moustache and rosy cheeks; extremely kind, and touchingly absorbed in the hobby of abolishing poverty and war.'

Gillette had a serious proposition. He wanted Sinclair to help him write a book which would clearly express his ideas. Sinclair was in fact already familiar with Gillette's work. In his autobiography he recalled that he had previously come across *World Corporation* and *Gillette's Social Redemption* on the shelves of the Pasadena Public Library some years earlier: 'I had taken them down and examined them with curiosity; they were written by a man who apparently had never read a Socialist book in his life but had thought it all out for himself.' Sinclair added that he guessed he was the only person who had ever opened the books.

Gillette's Social Redemption was actually written by Melvin Severy, of course, who had read many a Socialist book in his life, and it is likely that Sinclair was being a bit disingenuous about his mere passing knowledge of it. If he did peruse the book, he could hardly have failed to notice several references to Upton Sinclair in the index.

Sinclair told Gillette he could not help him, as he was midway through a book of his own. When Sinclair's wife Mary heard of the proposition, however, she wrote to Gillette and arranged to meet him herself. A woman of old-fashioned, genteel Southern manners, she too liked the elderly millionaire right away: 'I had never met anyone more lovable than this man who, when he was young, had worn out his shoes trying to find someone to manufacture and market his invention. He had never forgotten that once he was an underdog.' She persuaded her husband to help Gillette with his manuscript. They arranged that Gillette would spend two mornings a week with Sinclair discussing his ideas, paying the perpetually straitened novelist the sum of $500 a month for his services.

The Sinclairs soon discovered that King Gillette had a morbid fear of the word 'Socialism'. 'To him that meant class struggle and hatred,' wrote Sinclair. 'Whereas he insisted that his solution could all be brought about by gentle persuasion, and calm economic reasoning.'

Mrs Sinclair said that Gillette 'had heard about a man named Karl Marx who was a Socialist, but who had talked about confiscation and violence. Mr. Gillette had a horror of these.' Perhaps now it was Gillette who was being disingenuous. He had certainly not minded the word Socialism back in the days of *Twentieth Century* magazine, where advertisements for *The Human Drift* were printed alongside ads for *Das Kapital*. It was more likely that he now believed the term 'Socialism' would prejudice people against his corporate scheme. According to Mrs Sinclair, Gillette tried to get her husband to 'drop the

Socialist label and come over to the new dispensation'. Sinclair in turn tried to persuade the razor king that his 'corporationist' ideas were Socialist in all but name. The dispute was entirely semantic: officially, at least, neither of them was a Socialist. Upton Sinclair had recently quit the Socialist Party in order to support America's entry into the First World War, and King Camp Gillette, the self-described 'Discoverer of the Principles and Inventor of the System of "World Corporation"', was a registered Republican.

Sinclair thought Gillette should test his ideas out on some business people, and arranged a meeting at his house, inviting an oil man, a banker, a newspaper publisher, a lawyer and Mrs Kate Crane-Gartz, a plumbing heiress and a friend of Mary Sinclair. Gillette carefully explained to them the plan to which he had devoted so many years of thought, but he was not well received. 'By the time the session was over', wrote Mary Sinclair, 'the razor king had wilted like a flower on a cut stem; the perspiration stood out on his forehead and melted his collar.'

Gillette sent a letter to Sinclair shortly after this disastrous presentation, which had obviously shaken him. 'No more conferences for me of either labor or capital,' he wrote. 'I do not believe it tells anything whatever... I have met the type of men like your newspaper man and banker many, many times and they all travel in the same groove. And the groove is so deep, none of them ever see over the edge.'

Gillette and Sinclair continued to work on the manuscript, but Sinclair was becoming frustrated. If Gillette was well-meaning and sincere, he was also repetitive, insistent and a trifle needy. 'I discovered that the joy of his life was to get someone to listen while in his gentle pleading voice he told about his two-tome utopia,' said Sinclair. Gillette obviously found it difficult to allow his ideas to be presented by someone else, even under his close supervision. He would take away one of Sinclair's typewritten chapters and return it with dense pencilled notes and additions filling the margins and the spaces between lines. According to Mrs Sinclair, 'Mr Gillette tried to put the whole book into the first chapter; it was all so important, nothing of it could wait for the second.' In spite of Sinclair's sometimes patronising attitude towards the naive and kindly millionaire, it is clear that he believed in Gillette's system as a sort of all-American Socialism. 'King C Gillette, the razor man, has a plan for social reconstruction which I think is very remarkable,' he wrote to JG Phelps Stokes in 1919. 'I have been helping to get his manuscript into shape and have boiled it down to 110 typed pages.' But Gillette's voluminous revisions continued, and eventually Sinclair said he could do no more. According to Mary Sinclair, Gillette went away and got someone else to help him with his book. Gillette remained friends with the Sinclairs, however, and when his manuscript was finally finished Upton Sinclair convinced the New York publisher Horace Liveright to accept it – on the condition that Gillette paid for $25,000-worth of advertising. The result, which appeared in 1924, was called *The People's Corporation*.

Although Gillette's basic idea had changed little in the 30 years since the publication of *The Human Drift*, *The People's Corporation* is certainly the clearest statement of his aims. Whether or not a third party worked on the manuscript, Sinclair's influence is still evident. The writing is concise, passionate and deft. Particularly effective is Gillette's examination of the sheer waste and inefficiency of the profit system: 'We have the paradox of idle men, only too anxious for work, and idle plants in perfect condition for production, at the same time that people are starving and frozen. The reason is overproduction. It seems a bit absurd that when we have overproduced we should go without. One would think that overproduction would warrant a glorious holiday and a riot of feasting and display of all the superfluous goods lying around. On the contrary, overproduction produces want.'

The reviews, alas, were not good. 'Another Utopia, and to the mind of this reviewer the most hideous to date, which is saying much,' was *Outlook*'s verdict. In his review for the *Nation* Stuart Chase (who would one day coin the phrase 'New Deal' for FDR) did at least offer faint praise, describing Gillette's analysis of waste as 'soundly based and uniquely stated'. But even Chase was not beyond poking fun: 'The great world factory is full of torn belts, scaly boilers, broken gears, and unwashed windows. As a visiting stockholder, Mr Gillette makes the rounds of the plant, and his indignation knows no bounds. He pounds on the table and calls for the manager. There is no manager. What! No manager? Who runs this monstrosity? Nobody runs it; it runs itself. Good God, no wonder its inefficiency cries to heaven! And the man who has sold razors to hairy Ainos and Russian mujiks takes off his coat, clears the desk, opens the window, gets in a stenographer, and prepares to organize the business of feeding, clothing, sheltering, educating, and amusing the people of this planet.'

Despite the $25,000 advertising budget, which allowed for, among other things, a contest to 'Write your own review of *The People's Corporation*' with a top prize of $500, sales were poor. The audience which Gillette craved did not materialise, and his words of wisdom were heeded by no one.

Well, almost no one. A few years later a young Idaho vaudevillian named Glen Taylor was sitting in a relative's living room before dinner, idly perusing the volumes in a home-made bookcase. He pulled one down at random and began to read. 'That was the most fateful action of my life,' wrote Taylor in his 1979 memoirs. 'The rest of my life and the lives of untold numbers of other people would be affected, altered and made to flow in different channels because of that seemingly simple act.' The book was *The People's Corporation* by King Camp Gillette.

Taylor soon came to an uncut page, and asked his cousin's husband, a local Republican precinct committee man, for permission to cut it, having become utterly absorbed in the book's argument.

'You can have the goddamned thing if you want it,' replied his cousin-in-law. 'It's written by a bol-she-veeck.'

The book opened Taylor's eyes to the inequality of the present system, eventually steering him into politics. He ran for the US Senate, winning the Democratic nomination in 1940, and campaigning on a platform based on *The People's Corporation*. His opponents duly distributed some rather ominous-sounding extracts from the book, which were destined not to go down well in Idaho; selections such as: 'There will be no country towns, no individual farms, no fenced-in fields; there will be one vast sweep of land, divided into large tracts for production, and labor will be moved in organised bodies from one field of production to another.' Taylor lost in 1940, but he eventually did succeed in becoming a senator. In 1948 he joined the new Progressive Party as the running mate of Henry Wallace, the party's candidate for President of the United States. They received a million votes. King Gillette would never know that his book had ever so slightly changed the course of history.

**

'Failure in business is not a respecter of individuals, and strikes with equal indifference those at the lowest or highest round of the ladder of fortune,' Gillette wrote in *The Human Drift* in 1894, a year before he conceived of the invention that would one day make him a millionaire. Thirty years after he had penned those words, his fortune seemed impregnable enough, but the retired razor baron would live to see his own cruel assessment of capitalism finally proved right.

In 1925 he sent a postcard to the company's vice-president Frank Fahey from Hammerfest in Norway: 'This picture shows the most northern town in the world and Gillette razors are well represented.' While abroad he took his role as unofficial ambassador for the company seriously, paying calls on Gillette agents and visiting shops to inquire about sales. 'You would be surprised to see how interested these shopkeepers were,' he wrote to Fahey, 'when I let them know who I was.'

Most of the time he was recognised, of course, though his face had aged and his moustache whitened in the years since his trademark portrait was taken in 1906. On a visit to Egypt the portly razor magnate hoisted himself on to a camel for an inspection of the Pyramids. As the animal slowly got up off its knees, a crowd of locals gathered around Gillette, first pointing, then scraping their faces with hooked forefingers. The Gillette *Blade* recounted a story about a young gipsy musician in Spain who carried with him pictures of various crowned heads, among them the 'King of America', King Gillette, his royal portrait carefully cut from a packet of razor blades. In 1928 the French magazine *Fantasio* reported that an eccentric millionaire in Madrid had a statue of Gillette in his garden, 'the only great benefactor of humanity that we have had for 30 years'.

There is no doubt Gillette enjoyed the attention paid him, but his celebrity had an almost comical side to it that he probably failed to grasp. He was not known foremost as a business leader, or even a great inventor, but as an advertising icon. Indeed, many of those who met him had previously assumed that he was a fiction, a mere marketing creation designed to reinforce the Gillette brand. Meeting King C Gillette in the flesh was like being introduced to the Pillsbury Doughboy. He handed out sample blades and razors wherever he travelled, his good-natured public personality reduced to a promotional tool. A quarter of a century after the course of his life was altered by a fleeting inspiration, King Gillette had become a travelling salesman again, albeit one with more luggage.

As the Gillette Safety Razor Company celebrated its 25th anniversary, its founder could look back and claim that he had indeed changed the world, if not quite in the way he had intended when he first published *The Human Drift*. In 1926 the Gillette company was turning out 2.1 million blades a day, 100 miles of sharpened edge. Barbers had virtually given up shaving customers, and most sold Gillette blades in their shops. Gillette advertisements successfully promoted self-shaving as a masculine alternative to the 'ladylike massage-finish of the tonsorial artist.' In 1927 the *Blade* reprinted a 'tribute to the value of self-shaving by one of the world's outstanding exponents of efficiency and strenuosity', Benito Mussolini, proud owner of a gold Gillette DeLuxe shaving set.

Millions of servicemen had returned home from the war with government-issue Gillette razors (a few of them, as the *Blade* did not fail to report, had their lives saved when their field shaving sets stopped a bullet). Men across the world now shaved at home every day, in a fraction of the time their fathers once reserved for the operation. The notion of disposability was now part of American thinking, and the concept was intimately associated with the Gillette blade. Twenty seven years after King Gillette stood before his bathroom mirror with a dull safety razor in his hand, the hero of Sinclair Lewis's satirical novel *Babbitt* found himself in exactly the same situation:

> He hunted through the medicine-cabinet for a packet of new razor blades (reflecting, as invariably, 'Be cheaper to buy one of those dinguses and strop your own blades,') and when he discovered the packet, behind the round box of bicarbonate of soda, he thought ill of his wife for putting it there and very well of himself for not saying 'Damn'. But he did say it, immediately afterward, when with wet and soap-slippery fingers he tried to remove the horrible little envelope and crisp clinging oiled paper from the new blade.
>
> Then there was the problem, oft-pondered, never solved, of what to do with the old blade, which might imperil the fingers of his young. As usual, he tossed it on top of the medicine-cabinet, with a mental note that someday he must remove the 50 or 60 other blades that were also temporarily piled up there.

It was a good question: what *should* you do with your old blades? The idea that America wholeheartedly embraced the throwaway concept is undermined by the obvious difficulties people had in adjusting to it in this case. Several 'dinguses' came on the market designed to allow shavers to strop disposable blades in order to eke a few more shaves out of them. One Gillette imitator, the AutoStrop, came with a special attachment which allowed its single-edge blades to be stropped *in situ*. Some barbers even offered a re-sharpening service. Newspapers held contests asking for clever ways to dispose of dull blades, and consulted celebrities about what they did with theirs: HL Mencken insisted that he put them in the collection plate; in a 1927 magazine article King Gillette himself suggested men 'take them to be re-sharpened, and then never call for them'. People kept old blades to rip seams or cut tape; some soaked them in salt water or buried them until they rusted beyond threat, but simply throwing away something which seemed even marginally useful was actually deeply un-American, and took some getting used to. The remedy which finally prevailed says a great deal about the nation's ambivalent attitude towards the disposable dilemma: eventually most medicine cabinets were fitted with a slot for old blades that corresponded with a hole in the bathroom wall. The blades dropped into the dusty gap behind the plaster, where they multiplied over the years – out of sight, if not quite out of mind.

One might have expected that for Gillette, now an old man in his seventies, debates such as these would have lost their capacity to fascinate and absorb. On the contrary. In many ways, with his dreams of a corporate utopia evaporating, Gillette now made an extra effort to reclaim his razor blade as an achievement of real import to humankind. For him it seems the two projects were always related: both were, after all, inventions designed to eliminate wasted effort and increase efficiency.

Of his second invention, he said in 1921, 'A thing may be big or little, dependent on the perspective or background against which it is seen by each individual mind, whether it is looked upon in its individual sense, or in its collective sense.' The Gillette razor, he concluded, was a big thing, a world-shaping innovation: 'It will be found that there has never issued from the Patent Offices of the world any article of invention to meet an individual need, which has equalled or approached the Gillette Razor in its saving of time over the system it has displaced.' Performing the same sort of grand calculations that so captivated him while he worked out the numbers for his utopia, Gillette estimated that his razor saved mankind one-and-a-half billion dollars a year.

It had certainly made him a small fortune, which he now addressed himself to spending – mainly on more real estate. He purchased a plot in Pershing Square in downtown Los Angeles, with the intention of building a large office building on it. He acquired more acreage near Palm Springs and in Santa Barbara, but these were hardly reckless investments. The southern California property market was positively booming: in 1925 Gillette's chauffeur was able to quit his day job after making $732,200 by leasing a Beverly Hills lot he had purchased for $1,800.

In the late 1920s Gillette began construction of yet another home, a large, rambling mansion near Calabasas, in the Santa Monica mountains northwest of LA. The house was designed by Wallace Neff, a fashionable Los Angeles architect who also designed homes for Charlie Chaplin and Mary Pickford. As a teenager Walter Knapp worked on the Calabasas site. 'The place he had out there was just about like a castle,' says Knapp, now aged 90. 'It was built more or less on the mission style, but he had these blocks of adobe shipped in from Mexico.' When the house was nearly complete, Knapp's father, a skilled mason, was called in to build a large barbecue. Walter Knapp mixed mortar while the razor king inspected his new mock-Spanish palace, and was surprised by the down-to-earth manners of the millionaire: 'He was a real nice guy, for all the money he had and everything... a regular guy, just like you and I.'

Inevitably, there were people who sought to take advantage of Gillette's reputation in his old age. As his fame bled into the realms of myth, some even tried to claim credit for his most famous invention. In 1939 a southern California property developer named Howard Marr claimed in court that he had invented the Gillette razor and had been paid by Mr Gillette for it – by way of explaining where he got the initial capital to finance some questionable land deals. The lack of evidence aside, Marr's claim was not even marginally plausible: he had been 15 years old when the razor was first conceived.

Mr and Mrs King Gillette spent much of 1927 and 1928 abroad, while work at Calabasas continued, and costs mounted. Gillette, though still an extremely rich man, had already begun to over-extend himself financially. Mortgage payments, interest on loans, and huge tax bills tested his considerable liquidity. His health, too, was no longer as robust as it once was: he was plagued by high blood pressure and an intestinal complaint. But he was still in possession of 50,000 shares of Gillette stock, which in September 1929 was trading at upwards of $140 per share, a comfortable safety net worth approximately $7,000,000.

So it was in September. In October the stock market crashed, and both Gillette stock and California real estate plunged in value. Gillette had tried to sell some of his shares just prior to the crash, but the company's directors had talked him out of it, fearing bad publicity. Now it was too late. By November the value of Gillette stock was nearly halved. Worse still, the Gillette Safety Razor Company had further troubles, troubles that were nothing to do with the Depression.

King Gillette's original patents had expired in 1921, allowing anyone to make double-edged blades which would fit in the millions of Gillette razors in use across the globe. At the time the company's handling of the situation was widely admired – they slashed the price of the old razor set to a dollar, patented a new, five-dollar razor, and sold both side by side, reaping a fortune. Then Henry Jacques Gaisman stepped into the breach created by the patent expiration, the man who years before had invented the razor with the dingus that stropped the blades, the AutoStrop.

Gaisman, a prodigious inventor in the Gillette mould, came up with a double-edged blade with an unusually patterned perforation, which he dubbed the Probak. The Probak would fit in either a razor of his design or the Gillette razor, but Gillette blades would not fit in his handle. The Gillette company countered with a new razor design, and a blade which fitted both old and new Gillette razors, but not Gaisman's Probak. They announced the move in October 1929, but by November Gaisman was already turning out Probak blades by the mile, using the continuous strip process King Gillette had vainly attempted to introduce to his company many years earlier. When Gillette finally brought out its blade in January, Henry Gaisman claimed he had a prior patent on their design. Confident of its position, the Gillette Company issued an open invitation to anyone who thought he had an infringement case to seek redress in the courts. Gaisman accepted. Even as the lawyers squared off, merger talks between the two companies began, but Gillette stock was declining all the time under the strain of the litigation, fresh production difficulties and the discovery of financial irregularities during merger negotiations. When the company bought back 20,000 of King Gillette's 50,000 shares in order to facilitate the merger, he received only $1.6 million, barely enough to service his debts. He was lucky. In the months before the merger became final in November of 1930, Gillette common stock dipped below $30 a share.

In April 1931, as a result of the Gillette-AutoStrop merger, King Camp Gillette was forced to resign as president of the company, to make way for a new chief executive, Gerald Lambert, the man who had made Listerine a household name after discovering the obscure medical term 'halitosis' in a back number of the *Lancet*. Still a nominal director of the company he had founded, King Gillette was in ill health and plagued by mounting debt. Sales of property failed to cover the mortgages. In early 1930 his costly 40-year-old son King Gaines was sued for divorce by his wife Elizabeth. The *New York Times* reported that there had been 'a substantial property settlement'. The millionaire inventor was now beset on all sides by financial troubles. In a spectacular case of bad timing, Upton Sinclair started hitting him for money.

The Russian film director Sergei Eisenstein had come to America to make a picture for Paramount, an adaptation of Theodore Dreiser's novel *An American Tragedy*. That this collaboration never came to pass is not much of a surprise; indeed it is surprising that in the Red-baiting climate of the period it was even briefly considered. Eisenstein was not ready to go home, however, and approached Sinclair, seeking help in financing a film in Mexico. Sinclair set about raising money from his rich acquaintances. Kate Crane-Gartz, the plumbing heiress, put up an initial $5,000, but at least $25,000 was needed. Gillette, as a distant admirer of the Soviet experiment, was an obvious source for funding. It is unclear how much Gillette gave, although he must have given something, since Sinclair returned for more. Costs quickly rose as Eisenstein began shooting miles of film. And when he inquired about the possibility of further funds, Sinclair wrote with disappointing news: 'Mr Gillette told us that he had to sell some of his stock to pay his taxes...'

According to Sinclair, his only effort to introduce Gillette and Eisenstein failed; the Gillettes were not at home. In his memoirs, however, Eisenstein said different: 'I made the acquaintance of King Gillette, the inventor of the safety razor, when he was about 60.' It is difficult to imagine what might have transpired at a meeting between the razor king and the Russian director. Gillette was actually 76, and unwell. Eisenstein was just 33, mercurial and known to consort with, as the puritanical Sinclair put it, 'homos'. Of Gillette, Eisenstein said, 'He was obsessed with building villas in desert regions. A house – a palace – would rise above the sand; he would plant orchards all around it; but then the builder would dash off to a new part of the desert and build a new palace, and so on and so on.' The director recognised an unlikely kindred spirit in the old millionaire. 'I have lived much the same way, in relation to the events in my personal life,' he wrote, 'like a pack animal or horse that has a sheaf of corn hanging in front of him which he chases, headlong, hopelessly, forever.' It is a haunting image of Gillette at the end of his life, the failed utopian aimlessly constructing one little kingdom after another, then abandoning each in turn, leaving nothing but improved real estate in his wake.

As filming dragged on, Eisenstein wrote to Sinclair about the many species of cacti in the Mexican desert. 'I am glad for the cactus amateur, Mr King C Gillette, when he will see them on the screen. There are specimens never seen in California and Arizona, as to size, shape and beauty.'

But Gillette was never to see the cacti. His illness confined him mainly to his estate in Calabasas, where he desperately struggled to put his tangled affairs in some kind of order. In April 1932 he initiated a suit against his attorney Walter Hilborn (the son of one of the founding directors of the Gillette Safety Razor Company), alleging that Hilborn mismanaged an $8-million trust set up by Gillette, losing $1 million in the process. Gillette would not see this case come to trial. He died at Calabasas on 9 July 1932, with his wife and son at his bedside. He was buried in the private Gillette family room in the Forest Lawn mausoleum in Glendale, behind a plaque which bore his famous signature, King C Gillette.

In his will, revised the previous March, Gillette wrote: 'I am intentionally making no provision for my son, King G Gillette, in this will, having full faith and confidence in my said wife to make such provision for our said son as she may deem best.' This precaution was ultimately unnecessary, since the remainder of Gillette's portfolio, worth about $1 million, was soon absorbed by creditors. The Calabasas house was sold for a fraction of what it had cost to build. Within a few years everything was gone.

***

Glen Taylor, the senator from Idaho and the closest thing Gillette ever had to a disciple, would finally describe Gillette's social vision as 'a beautiful pipe dream. It won't work because people just aren't built that way.' This is probably as fair a summation of the razor king's contribution to American political life as any. Even his most radical ideas were derivative, and his 'industrial solution' seemed to combine all the least plausible elements of socialism, technocracy and the utopian prognostications of Bellamy and others.

It would be too simplistic to describe King Gillette as a man of contradictions, though he was that. The author who advocated a world free of privilege and class distinction was not only rich; he was also a 32nd degree Freemason, and a member of no less than five prestigious clubs. The scourge of all those who used their capital to live off the work of others did just that for the last part of his life, spending as prodigiously as his income would allow. The outspoken critic of the Homestead Act as a wasteful means of squandering the nation's wealth himself acquired government property under the Desert Land Act, a similar scheme which dispensed acreage cheaply to anyone promising to irrigate it. He never gave up on the corporation as a utopian model, though he had experienced its manifold inadequacies first hand. He was, however, more than just another plutocrat with an axe to grind, like Henry Ford. Ultimately, Gillette was a man who travelled two roads at once, with one foot on earth and one in a heaven-on-earth of his own design.

The contradiction is a quintessentially American one.

During Gillette's lifetime the country was not unfamiliar with millionaire socialists and inventor-philosophers. Gillette is one of many who combined a sincere wish for a better world with an inventive flair which just suited the deeply flawed present. His weird socialist friend Melvin Severy filed patents with as much verve as Gillette. The pioneering scientist Charles Steinmetz, a contemporary of Gillette, developed similar ideas about the corporation as the model for a co-operative society while toiling in his laboratory at General Electric. Even Henry David Thoreau, whose essays on nature and individualism were the antithesis of corporate, consumerist America, had previously invented several new processes in pencil manufacturing which allowed his family's business to dominate the American market. There is another, more poignant connection between Gillette and Thoreau: the author of *Civil Disobedience*, who famously retreated to the banks of Walden Pond in 1845, ten years before King Gillette was born, did so initially as a tribute to his beloved elder brother John, who had died of blood poisoning 11 days after cutting himself with a straight razor.

Acknowledgements

I am indebted to Walter Knapp for sharing his personal memories of King Gillette, and to Thomas Sci, who allowed me to borrow an original Gillette razor from the front window of his barber-shop in Darien, Connecticut. For their invaluable and generous assistance I would also like to thank Sophie de Brant and Piers Feltham, and Melissa, Lynn and Chris Dowling.

Select Bibliography

King Camp Gillette: *The Human Drift* (Scholars' Facsimiles & Reprints, Inc, introd. by Kenneth M Roemer, 1976); *World Corporation* (New England News, 1910); *The People's Corporation* (Boni and Liveright,1924); 'Origin of the Gillette Razor', *The Gillette Blade*, February & March 1918
William Nickerson: 'The Development of the Gillette Safety Razor', *The Gillette Blade*, May 1918-January 1919
Russell B Adams, Jr: *King C Gillette - The Man and His Wonderful Shaving Device* (Little Brown, 1978)
Upton Sinclair: *The Autobiography of Upton Sinclair* (Harcourt, Brace & World, 1962)
Mary Craig Sinclair: *Southern Belle* (Sinclair Press, 1957)

Born in Connecticut in 1963, Tim Dowling is a journalist and columnist. He lives in London with his wife and three sons.